INSTANT POT COOKBOOK

Quick and Easy Recipes for Your Homemade Meals

Written by: Emma Brown

DEDICATION:

This recipe book is dedicated to **S.Yushko**, a big fan of Instant Pot Pressure Cooker☺.

Table of Contents

INTRODUCTION

I want to congratulate you for having the book, "Instant Pot Cookbook: Quick and Easy Recipes for Your Homemade Meals".

Food is the primary need of every creature, including human beings. It is the first way of people to survive. No matter how old are you, you need food to continue your life. Children need food to grow while the older ones need food intake to survive and stay healthy. However, not only the quantity of food but the quality of food consumed is also necessary to consider.

In our grandma era people ate healthy food. They had a good combination of healthy good quality ingredients and healthy way of cooking. This made a perfect food that contains essential nutrient for the body. An excellent composition between carbohydrates, vitamin, and protein is the best fuel for the body to stay strong and healthy.

Nevertheless, as the time passed by, people start to change. Too often having not enough time and being busy all the time make people forget to consume good quality of food. They begin to have any kind of fast food that is easy to grab and consume. Besides the flexibility of fast food—can be eaten any time and anywhere, it can't be denied that fast food tastes good as well. Everyone will agree that French fries, burgers, and instant noodles are delicious. However, do fast food offer good nutrition content?

Though fast food seems to be the perfect solution for those who are busy, it should be realized that fast food doesn't provide enough nutrition needed by the body. Moreover, there is a big danger behind that mouthwatering fast food as it contains high carbohydrates and cholesterol, which are bad for the body.

So, if living longer with a healthy body is your dream, you have to start considering the healthier way of eating, no matter you like it or not.

8 Benefits of Having Homemade Meals

Cooking at home is almost impossible in this modern era. Considering the fact that it needs more time, equipment, and other extra efforts, people prefer to eat in the restaurant to having a homemade food. However, there are several benefits of eating homemade food that will make you think twice eating outside.

- **It saves money.**

  Eating homemade is absolutely cheaper than eating in the restaurant. If you eat at the restaurant, surely you don't spend money for food only, but we also pay the staff, electricity, buildings, water, and much more.

- **It is healthier.**

  If you prepare your own meal from home, you will know exactly the ingredients you put in your meal. You can adjust and plan the healthiest ingredients that will go to your body. This is very good for your diet, isn't it?

- **It avoids allergic.**

  If your beloved and you are being sensitive to certain ingredients, you may easily avoid them if you cook the meals by yourselves. It will reduce the risk of allergic reaction that will discomfort your beloved and you.

- **It controls the portion.**

  Oftentimes, restaurants serve portions that are larger than your need. The problem is, when the food is in front of you, it will be difficult not to eat it. If you cook the food yourselves, you will be able to control the amount of food served on your tables and eliminate unnecessary temptation.

- **It brings family togetherness**.

  Eating at home offers you a chance to spend more time with your beloved. You don't need to waste your time for traffic jams and busy roads. Besides, you can involve your beloved in preparing the food. This will create a bonding that will strengthen your relationship.

- **It improves your knowledge of food.**

  Cooking will not only give you knowledge on how to fill up your stomach and satisfy your tongue, but it also teaches you about the food content and how it influences your body. You will be experienced on how to combine nutritious food to satisfy your craving.

- **It ensures the cleanliness of the food.**

  By cooking your meal at your kitchen, you will not only know how healthy it is, but you will also ensure how clean it is. Naturally, you will keep your cooking equipment clean and sterile.

- **It increases creativity.**

  Cooking at home makes it possible for you to have extraordinary food. You can easily put some ingredients and create new dishes. You will be satisfied to eat some meals with your favorite ingredients.

An Instant Pot: The Best Partner in the Kitchen

It can't be denied that having homemade meals offer a lot of advantages. However, cooking seems to be impossible for some people. Many people are not confidence enough to serve homemade meals while some others think that cooking will spend much of their time. The question is: Is it possible to serve scrumptious and healthy food from home with a minimum skill and time?

Fortunately, there is a new technique called Instant Pot. An Instant Pot is coming as the answer for those who want to cook but doesn't have a lot of time. By using this Instant Pot, you will be able to serve delicious food for your breakfast, lunch, and dinner without messing up your daily activities.

An Instant Pot is a programmable pressure cooker that has multi-functions in one. It is really a multi-function cooking equipment that is completed with ability as a pressure cooker, slow cooker, rice cooker, sauté pan, steamer, warmer, and yogurt maker. It magically minimizes all your kitchen equipment in one pot.

Here are 10 Reasons Why You Should Use an Instant Pot:

- **It saves times and energy.**
  An Instant Pot saves lots of your time and energy, as it only needs minimum time to cook many kinds ingredients that usually need hour's treatment. An Instant Pot takes 30-40 minutes to cook a beef stew—a shorter time comparing with a slow cooker that needs 4-8 hours in cooking the same meals.
- **It is a super assistant.**
  Completed with 7 function—as a pressure cooker, slow cooker, rice cooker, sauté pan, steamer, warmer, and yogurt maker, an Instant is really your diligent assistant at the kitchen.
- **It serves healthier and tastier meal.**
  As an Instant Pot doesn't need a lot of time to cook, it serves food with the best flavor while still retaining the nutrients.
- **It is easy to use.**

Having 7 appliances in your kitchen sounds so complicated, right? An Instant Pot can do it all. You just have to press a few buttons and walk away. The food will be ready in a few minutes with delicious taste.

- **It is safe.**
  Even your children can use it. They don't have to cook with fire. Automatically, this reduces the burning risk.

- **It is convenient.**
  By having an Instant Pot, you don't need to stay in front of the stove. The pressure cooker will cook your food then automatically warm it if you want to consume it later.

- **It is comfortable.**
  Cooking using a stove with its heat and sweat is not fun. It feels like staying in the oven than a kitchen. An Instant Pressure Cooker helps you to cook with no steam, sweat, noise, and smell. Your kitchen will be completely neat.

- **It doesn't need to defrost the ingredients.**
  Sometimes you went home late and find that you still have to thaw some meat for dinner. An Instant Pot can cook any kind of ingredients right away from the freezer. You don't need to waste your time for thawing and other useless cooking activities.

- **It has great size.**
  An Instant Pot comes in various sizes. No matter you are single, couples, or a family of four, there is several sizes of Instant Pot that you can use. All of the Instant Pot has the same functions.

- **It is affordable.**
  Imagine if you have to buy a lot of appliances for your kitchen. Surely, you will say that an Instant Pot is affordable.

Lucky you, this book provide with many recipes that you can use to prepare a delicious meal by using an Instant Pot. Completed with breakfast, lunch, and dinner recipes to help you create a healthy menu for a full month. BON APPETIT!

BREAKFAST

Pork and Egg Burritos

(Ready in about 30 minutes | Servings 3)

Ingredients

¼ cup ground pork

½ teaspoon salt

¼ teaspoon ground black pepper

½ teaspoon thyme

½ teaspoon sage

½ teaspoon red pepper flakes

1-teaspoon brown sugar

¼ teaspoon nutmeg

1-teaspoon olive oil

3 tortillas

4 fresh eggs

2 tablespoons fresh milk

½ teaspoon pepper

Directions

Pour water in the pressure cooker the place a trivet in it.

Wrap the tortilla sheets with aluminum foil then set aside.

Place ground pork in a bowl then season with salt, black pepper, thyme, sage, red pepper flakes, brown sugar, and nutmeg. Stir them well until the pork is completely seasoned.

Cover the bowl with plastic wrap then chills the seasoned pork in the refrigerator for about 15 minutes.

Crack the eggs then place in an oven safe bowl.

Add milk and pepper into the eggs then whisk until incorporated.

Remove the seasoned pork from the refrigerator then put it in the egg mixture.

Using a wooden spatula, slowly stir the pork with the eggs until become small pieces.

Cover the bowl with aluminum foil then place on the trivet inside the pressure cooker.

Place the wrapped tortilla on the bowl then cover the pressure cooker with the lid.

Press the "Manual" button then set time for 12 minutes.

Once it is done, naturally release the pressure cooker then remove the tortilla and the bowl.

Unwrap the tortillas and place on a flat surface.

Take about 3 scoops of cooked pork and egg then drop on the tortilla. Repeat to the remaining tortillas.

Roll each tortilla tightly then enjoy right away.

Beef and Cheese Quiche

(Ready in about 45 minutes | Servings 2)

Ingredients

3 fresh eggs

4 tablespoons fresh milk

A pinch of salt

A pinch of black pepper

1-cup ground beef

½ cup grated mozzarella cheese

½ cup chopped onion

Directions

Place a trivet in a pressure cooker then add 1-½ cups of water.

Prepare a medium soufflé dish then grease with cooking oil. Set aside.

Crack the eggs then place in a bowl. Add fresh milk, salt, and black pepper in it then whisk until fluffy.

Add the ground beef, mozzarella cheese, and chopped onion into the egg mixture then stir well.

Pour the mixture into the prepared soufflé dish and cover with aluminum foil.

Place in the pressure cooker then cover with the lid properly.

Cook for 30 minutes on high pressure and once it is done, turn it off and quick release the pressure cooker.

Open the lid carefully then remove the dish from the pressure cooker.

Discard the aluminum foil then serve and enjoy.

Strawberry Lemon Oats

(Ready in about 15 minutes | Servings 1)

Ingredients

1-½ teaspoons margarine

½ cup oats

1-½ cups water

3 teaspoons sugar

1 teaspoon lemon zest

½ cup fresh strawberries

2 tablespoons chia seeds

Directions

Put margarine in a pressure cooker pot then choose the sauté button.

Once it is melted, add the oat then stir for approximately 3 minutes—the oat will smell nutty.

Pour water into the pot together with sugar and lemon zest then cover with the lid and cook for 5 minutes on high pressure.

Once it is done, carefully release the pressure cooker, open the lid then add strawberry and chia seeds.

Cook uncover for about 5 minutes then transfer the oats to a serving cup.

Serve and enjoy immediately.

Original Baked Potatoes

(Ready in about 30 minutes | Servings 2)

Ingredients

4 medium potatoes

3 teaspoons butter

¼ teaspoon salt

½ teaspoon black pepper

Directions

Wash the potatoes properly then pricks using a fork.

Pour a cup of water in a pressure cooker then place a trivet in it.

Arrange the potatoes on the trivet then close the pressure cooker properly.

Select the high-pressure button then select time for 12 minutes.

When the beep sounds, turn it off then naturally release the pressure cooker.

Meanwhile, preheat an oven to 400 °F and line a baking pan with aluminum foil.

Transfer the potatoes to the baking pan then bake for about 10 minutes.

Once it is done, remove from the oven then arrange the baked potatoes on a serving dish.

Brush with butter then sprinkle salt and black pepper on top. Enjoy!

Pumpkin Cake with Cinnamon Sauce

(Ready in about 30 minutes | Servings 4)

Ingredients

6 fresh eggs

3 tablespoons palm sugar

3 tablespoons butter

¾ cup pumpkin puree

6 tablespoons yogurt

1-teaspoon vanilla extract

1-cup wheat flour

2 tablespoons multi-purpose flour

1-teaspoon baking powder

2 teaspoons cinnamon

1-teaspoon pumpkin pie spice

1-cup raisins

SAUCE

¾ cup plain yogurt

3 tablespoons honey

1-teaspoon cinnamon

¼ teaspoon vanilla extract

Directions

Place butter in a saucepan over low heat. Once it melts, remove from heat then set aside.

Prepare a 7-inch spring form pan then greases with cooking spray.

Place eggs and sugar in a mixing bowl then using an electric mixer beat them until smooth and fluffy.

Add pumpkin puree together with yogurt and vanilla extract. Continue beating until combined well.

In a separate bowl, place the flour; baking powder and pumpkin pie spice then stir well.

Add the flour mixture into the liquid mixture then slowly stir using a wooden spatula.

Fold in the raisins then pour the batter into the prepared spring form pan.

14

Pour water into a pressure cooker and put a trivet in it.

Place the spring form pan on the trivet then cover the pressure cooker properly.

Select the high-pressure menu then cook for 30 minutes.

Meanwhile, combine all of the sauce ingredients in a bowl then stir well.

Once the cake is cooked, naturally release the pressure cooker.

After 10 minutes, open the lid and remove the cake and let it cool for a few minutes.

Transfer the cake to a serving dish then drizzle the cinnamon sauce on top.

Serve and enjoy.

Light Chicken Soup

(Ready in about 25 minutes | Servings 2)

Ingredients

½ lb. chicken thigh	½ teaspoon pepper
½ cup chopped carrots	¼ teaspoon nutmeg
½ cup potato cubes	½ teaspoon salt
1 tablespoon chopped leek	2 teaspoon fried shallot
2 tablespoons chopped onion	2 cups water

Directions

Place chicken thighs, chopped carrots, and potato cubes in the pressure cooker pot.

Add onion, pepper, salt, and nutmeg into the pot then pour water over the thighs. Stir well.

Cover the pressure cooker with the lid and seal properly.

Select the menu to high and set the time to 15 minutes.

When the beeps sounds, naturally release the pressure cooker then open the lid.

Add chopped leek into the pot then cook uncover for approximately 5 minutes.

Transfer the hot soup to a serving bowl then sprinkle fried shallots on top.

Serve and enjoy hot!

LUNCH

Steamed Fish Tomato

(Ready in about 15 minutes | Servings 2)

Ingredients

½ lb. fish fillet

1-cup cherry tomatoes

½ cup olives

1 teaspoon minced garlic

A pinch of salt

A pinch of pepper

½ cup water

Directions

Cut the cherry tomatoes into halves. Set aside.

Pour water into a pressure cooker then preheat the pressure cooker.

Place fish fillet into the pressure cooker pot then sprinkle halved cherry tomatoes, minced garlic, and olives over the fish fillet.

Cover the pressure cooker with the lid and seal tightly.

Select the menu to low pressure and cook for about 7 minutes.

Once it is done, naturally release the pressure cooker then open the lid.

Transfer the steamed fish together with the tomatoes to a serving dish then dust with salt and pepper.

Serve and enjoy warm.

Beef Cheese Sandwich

(Ready in about 30 minutes | Servings 2)

Ingredients

1 lb. roasted beef

½ teaspoon salt

1-teaspoon black pepper

3 teaspoons Worcestershire sauce

1 teaspoon minced garlic

1-teaspoon garlic powder

½ cup beef broth

½ cup mozzarella cheese

2 buns

Directions

Cut the roasted beef into small chunks then place in a pressure cooker pot.

Season with salt, black pepper, Worcestershire sauce, minced garlic, and garlic powder then pours beef broth in it.

Cover and seal the pressure cooker properly then cook for 15 minutes on high pressure.

Naturally, release the pressure cooker then open the lid.

Stir the beef occasionally then remove from the pressure cooker.

Cut the buns horizontally then place cooked beef inside and add mozzarella cheese.

Toast the bread for about 2 minutes—just until the mozzarella cheese melts.

Serve and enjoy.

Zucchini Soup

(Ready in about 20 minutes | Servings 4)

Ingredients

1-tablespoon olive oil	½ teaspoon pepper
2 onions	5 cups water
2 teaspoons minced garlic	¼ cup yogurt
3 cups chopped zucchini	¼ cup sour cream
½ teaspoon salt	¼ cup grated cheese

Directions

Peel and chop the onions then place in a pressure cooker pot.

Add chopped zucchini and minced garlic then season with salt and pepper.

Pour 5 cups water and splash olive oil into the pot.

Close the pressure cooker with the lid and seal properly.

Select the menu to high pressure and set time to 5 minutes.

Naturally, release the pressure cooker then open the lid.

Transfer the soup to a blender then add yogurt and sour cream in it.

Blend until smooth and creamy then pour into a serving bowl.

Sprinkle grated cheese on top then serve warm.

Pork Meatball BBQ

(Ready in about 15 minutes | Servings 2)

Ingredients

1 lb. ground pork	¼ cup breadcrumbs
1-teaspoon pepper	1 egg
½ teaspoon salt	1-tablespoon olive oil
1-tablespoon cornstarch	1 cup BBQ sauce

Directions

Place ground beef in a bowl then season with pepper and salt.

Add cornstarch, breadcrumbs, and egg into the bowl then mix until well combined.

Shape the mixture into medium meatballs then set aside.

Place olive oil and BBQ sauce into the pressure cooker pot then stir well.

Arrange the meatballs in the pot then cover the pressure cooker with the lid.

Cook on high pressure for 5 minutes then naturally release the pressure cooker.

Once it is done, remove the meatballs from the pressure cooker then transfer to a serving dish.

Serve and enjoy.

Sweet Mixed Beans in Black Pepper

(Ready in about 45 minutes | Servings 4)

Ingredients

½ cup navy beans

½ cup pinto beans

½ cup chopped bacon

2 tablespoons chopped onion

1 teaspoon minced garlic

1-cup water

½ cup beef broth

2 tablespoons sugar

¼ teaspoon salt

1-teaspoon black pepper

1 teaspoon Dijon mustard

Directions

Place the navy beans and pinto beans in a bowl then soak overnight.

Discard the water then rinse the beans. Set aside.

Select the pressure cooker to sauté menu.

Stir in chopped bacon the sauté until crisp and aromatic then add minced garlic and chopped onion.

Pour beef broth and water into the pot then add the beans into the pot.

Season with sugar, salt, black pepper, and Dijon mustard then seal the pressure cooker properly.

Select the menu to the high pressure cooker and set time to 35 minutes.

Once the beep sounds, naturally release the pressure cooker and let it comes down.

Open the lid then transfer the cooked beans to a serving dish.

Serve and enjoy.

Energizing Beef and Veggie

(Ready in about 45 minutes | Servings 2)

Ingredients

1-½ lbs. beef brisket

1-cup water

¼ cup chopped onion

½ teaspoon black pepper

¼ teaspoon salt

½ lb. potato

½ cup chopped carrot

1 cup chopped cabbage

Directions

Place the beef brisket in a pressure cooker pot then season with onion, pepper, and salt.

Seal the pressure cooker properly and cook for 20 minutes.

Once it is done, quick release the pressure cooker then open the lid.

Next, peel and cut the potato into wedges then toss into the pressure cooker together with chopped carrot and cabbage.

Close the lid then select the menu to high and set time to 5 minutes.

When the beep sounds, naturally release the pressure cooker then open the lid.

Transfer the cooked beef and vegetables to a serving dish.

Serve and enjoy.

DINNER

Delicious Spicy Cabbage

(Ready in about 20 minutes | Servings 2)

Ingredients

1-½ teaspoons sesame oil

1-½ lbs. cabbage

¼ cup grated carrots

¾ cup water

2 tablespoons apple cider vinegar

½ teaspoon granulated sugar

¼ teaspoon cayenne

¼ teaspoon red pepper flakes

1-teaspoon cornstarch

Directions

Cut the cabbage into wedges then place in a pressure cooker pot.

Pour sesame oil over the cabbage wedges then select the menu to sauté. Stir until brown.

Add grated carrots into the pot then season the vegetables with cayenne, apple cider vinegar, sugar, and red pepper flakes.

Pour water over the vegetables then cover the pressure cooker properly.

Select the menu to high then set the time for 5 minutes.

Once it is done, naturally release the pressure cooker.

When the pressure cooker is cooler, open the lid then take the vegetables out from the pot.

Arrange the cooked cabbage and carrot on a serving dish. Set aside.

Take about ¼ cup of the liquid then mix with cornstarch.

Return the mixture into the pot then bring to a simmer until the liquid become thick.

Pour the sauce over the cooked cabbage and carrots then serve right away.

Tomato Mushroom Risotto

(Ready in about 15 minutes | Servings 2)

Ingredients

1 ½ teaspoons olive oil

¼ cup chopped onion

1 cup Arborio rice

2 tablespoons wine

½ cup chopped mushroom

2 cups vegetable broth

1 ½ teaspoons tomato paste

A pinch of salt

Directions

Choose the sauté menu in the pressure cooker then place onion with olive oil in the pot. Stirring occasionally until brown.

Toss in Arborio rice and splash wine over then stir until the rice completely absorbs the wine.

Pour vegetable broth into the pot then add the remaining ingredients into the pot.

Put the lid on the pressure cooker then close properly.

Select the menu to high and set the time to 5 minutes.

When the beep sounds, turn it off then naturally release the pressure cooker.

Carefully open the lid then stirs the cooked rice.

Transfer the cooked rice to a serving dish then enjoy warm.

Lentils Spiced Soup

(Ready in about 20 minutes | Servings 2)

Ingredients

1-cup lentils

2 cups chopped spinach

2 tablespoons lemon juice

4 cups water

A pinch of pepper

3 teaspoons margarine

1 ½ teaspoon olive oil

¼ cup chopped onion

½ teaspoon garlic powder

1-teaspoon coriander

¼ teaspoon cinnamon

¼ teaspoon turmeric

¼ teaspoon cayenne

¼ teaspoon nutmeg

½ teaspoon salt

Directions

Select the sauté menu in the pressure cooker then place margarine and olive oil into the pot.

Once it is melted, stir in onion, garlic, and all of the spices into the pot then sauté occasionally until aromatic.

Pour water over the spices then add in lentils.

Cover the pressure cooker with its lid and close properly.

Cook for 10 minutes on high then quick release the pressure cooker.

After the pressure cooker comes down, open the lid then put the spinach into the pot.

Stir occasionally—the spinach will naturally be soft as the soup is still hot.

Transfer the soup to a serving bowl then splash lemon juice over the soup.

Serve and enjoy hot.

Beef Stew with Black Pepper

(Ready in about 25 minutes | Servings 2)

Ingredients

1-tablespoon olive oil

1 lb. beef

½ teaspoon rosemary

¼ cup chopped onion

2 tablespoons chopped celery

4 tablespoons red wine

1-cup beef broth

¼ teaspoon salt

A pinch of black pepper

¼ cup chopped carrots

3 teaspoons butter

3 teaspoons multi-purpose flour

Directions

Cut the beef into cubes then place in a pressure cooker pot.

Sauté the beef together with olive oil until wilted then stir in chopped onion, rosemary, salt, pepper, and chopped celery.

Pour beef stock into the pot then close the pressure cooker with the lid and seal properly.

Cook on high pressure for 15 minutes then naturally release the pressure cooker.

Open the lid then add chopped carrots into the pot then stir well.

Meanwhile, preheat a saucepan then melt butter in it.

Once it is melted, add in flour and stir until become paste.

Take about ¼ cup of the gravy and pour over the saucepan. Stir until dissolved.

Return the butter and gravy mixture into the pot, stir occasionally then bring to boil for approximately 5 minutes.

Transfer the beef stew to a serving dish then serve warm.

Chicken in Tomato

(Ready in about 20 minutes | Servings 2)

Ingredients

1 lb. chicken drumsticks

½ cup chicken broth

1-cup tomato puree

¼ cup chopped onion

½ teaspoon garlic powder

½ teaspoon oregano

1 bay leaf

A pinch of salt

Directions

Place chicken drumsticks, chopped onion, oregano, garlic powder, bay leaf, salt, and tomato puree in a pressure cooker pot the pour chicken broth into the pot.

Cover the pressure cooker with the lid then set the menu to high and select the time to 15 minutes.

Once it is done, naturally release the pressure cooker and let it comes down for a few minutes.

Open the pressure cooker, then take the cooked chicken out from the pressure cooker and arrange on a serving dish.

Pour the tomato sauce over the chicken then serve right away.

Salmon in Tropical Sauce

(Ready in about 20 minutes | Servings 2)

Ingredients

2 lbs. salmon fillet

1-cup pineapple chunks

1 lemon

1 onion

1 tablespoon chopped parsley

1-tablespoon olive oil

¼ teaspoon salt

¼ teaspoon pepper

Directions

Pour water into the pressure cooker then place a steamer basket inside.

Cut the onion into wedges then set aside.

Lay aluminum foil on a flat surface then place salmon fillet on it.

Brush olive oil on the salmon then season with salt and pepper.

Sprinkle pineapple chunks, onion wedges, and chopped parsley over the salmon then splash lemon juice.

Wrap the salmon and other ingredients then place on the pressure cooker steamer basket.

Close the pressure cooker and seal properly.

Set the menu to high and cook for 12 minutes.

Once it is done, naturally release the pressure cooker and open the lid.

Remove the cooked salmon from the pressure cooker, unwrap, and place on a serving dish.

Serve and enjoy.

Warm Fish Ginger

(Ready in about 15 minutes | Servings 2)

Ingredients

1 lb. fish fillet

¼ cup orange juice

1 teaspoon orange zest

1 teaspoon ginger powder

½ cup chopped onion

1-tablespoon olive oil

¼ teaspoon salt

¼ teaspoon pepper

1-cup fish broth

Directions

Brush olive oil over the fish fillet then season with salt and pepper. Set aside for about 10 minutes.

Meanwhile, place chopped onion, ginger powder, and orange zest into the pressure cooker pot.

Pour fish broth and orange juice into the pot then stir well.

Add the seasoned fish into the pot then cover the pressure cooker properly.

Select the menu to high then set the time to 5 minutes.

When the beep sounds, naturally release the pressure cooker then open the lid.

Transfer the fish and the gravy to a serving dish. Serve and enjoy!

DESSERT AND SWEETS

Brown Bread Pudding

(Ready in about 30 minutes | Servings 4)

Ingredients

¼ cup butter

½ cup palm sugar

3 cups almond milk

3 eggs

1-teaspoon vanilla extract

½ teaspoon cinnamon

¼ teaspoon salt

8 slices bread

½ cup raisins

¼ cup chopped pecans

Directions

Prepare a pressure cooker proof dish then cover with aluminum foil.

Pour water into the pressure cooker then place a trivet inside.

Preheat a saucepan then melts the butter.

Once it is melted, pour the butter into a bowl then combine with palm sugar, almond milk, eggs, vanilla extract, salt, and cinnamon. Whisk until incorporated.

Cut the bread into cubes then add into the butter mixture together with raisins.

Let it sit for about 20 minutes until the milk mixture is completely absorbed by the bread.

Pour the mixture into the prepared dish then sprinkle chopped pecans over the bread.

Place the dish on the trivet then seal the pressure cooker properly.

Select high-pressure menu and set the time to 20 minutes.

Once it is done, naturally release the pressure cooker open the lid.

Remove the bread pudding from the pressure cooker then let it cool for a few minutes.

Serve and enjoy.

New York Cheesecake

(Ready in about 60 minutes | Servings 4)

Ingredients

CRUST:

¾ cup graham crackers

1 tablespoon granulated sugar

2 tablespoons unsalted butter

FILLING:

1-cup cream cheese

½ cup granulated sugar

½ tablespoon multi-purpose flour

½ teaspoon vanilla extract

½ teaspoon orange zest

½ teaspoon lemon zest

1 egg yolk

4 tablespoons whipping cream

TOPPING:

½ cup plain yogurt

½ tablespoon granulated sugar

Directions

Make the crust. Prepare a cheesecake pan then grease with cooking spray.

Place graham crackers and sugar in a food processor then process until becoming small crumbs.

Place butter in a saucepan then melts over very low heat.

Add melted butter into the crackers mixture then mix well.

Place the crust into the prepared cheesecake pan then press completely.

Freeze the crust for approximately 15 minutes.

Make the filling. Place cream cheese in a mixing bowl then beat until smooth and creamy.

Crack the egg then place in the cream cheese mixture. Continue stirring until well combined.

Pour the mixture into the pizza crust and spread evenly.

Pour water into a pressure cooker then put a trivet inside.

Place the cheesecake on the trivet. Close the pressure cooker with its lid then seal properly.

Select the menu to high pressure and set the time to 35 minutes.

Once it is done, naturally release the pressure cooker and let the pressure cooker comes down.

Open the lid then remove the cheesecake from the pressure cooker.

Make the topping. Combine yogurt and sugar in a bowl then stir until incorporated.

Spread over the top of the Cheesecake and let them cool.

Keep in the refrigerator for at least 4 hours or overnight.

Serve and enjoy cool.

Caramel Baked Apple

(Ready in about 25 minutes | Servings 2)

Ingredients

2 apples

2 tablespoons raisins

½ cup red wine

4 tablespoons granulated sugar

½ teaspoon cinnamon

Directions

Core the apples then place on the bottom of a pressure cooker.

Add granulated sugar and raisins into the pot then pour red wine over the apples.

Dust cinnamon on top then seal the pressure cooker properly.

Select the menu to high pressure and select the time to 10 minutes.

Once it is done, naturally release the pressure cooker then open the lid.

Remove the apples and the liquid from the pressure cooker then place in a serving dish.

Serve and enjoy.

Almond Rice Pudding

(Ready in about 20 minutes | Servings 2)

Ingredients

½ cup Arborio rice

2-½ cups almond milk

½ cup water

½ teaspoon cinnamon

1 teaspoon orange zest

1-cup condensed milk

2 tablespoons honey

½ cup roasted almond

Directions

Place Arborio rice in a pressure cooker pot then pours almond milk and water in it.

Add cinnamon and orange zest into the Arborio rice and stir well.

Cover the pressure cooker and seal properly then cook on high-pressure for 15 minutes.

Once it is done, naturally release the pressure cooker and open the lid.

Pour condensed milk over the rice then mix until combined.

Transfer the cooked Arborio rice to a serving dish and let it cool for a few minutes.

Drizzle honey over the rice then sprinkle roasted almonds on top.

Serve and enjoy.

Lemon Crème Brulée

(Ready in about 25 minutes | Servings 3)

Ingredients

4 egg yolks

6 tablespoons granulated sugar

1-cup heavy cream

1 ½ teaspoon lemon juice

Directions

Pour water into the pressure cooker then place a trivet in it.

Place egg yolks, 3 tablespoons granulated sugar, heavy cream, and lemon juice in a bowl. Whisk until incorporated.

Strain the mixture then divide into 3 custard cups. Cover the cup with aluminum foil then arrange on the trivet.

Close and seal the pressure cooker then cook on high pressure for 6 minutes.

Naturally, release the pressure cooker then open the lid.

Remove the cups into a serving tray. Sprinkle the remaining sugar on the top then serve and enjoy.

Sweet Caramel Flan

(Ready in about 25 minutes | Servings 2)

Ingredients

CARAMEL:

4 tablespoons granulated sugar

1-tablespoon water

CUSTARD:

1 egg

1 egg yolk

2 tablespoons granulated sugar

¾ cup fresh milk

3 tablespoons whipped cream

½ teaspoon vanilla extract

3 teaspoons maple syrup

Directions

Pour water into a pressure cooker then place a trivet inside. Set aside.

Place the caramel ingredients in a saucepan over very low heat. Bring to boil.

Swirl the saucepan gently then once the sugar is caramelized, pour into two custard cups. Set aside.

Combine egg and egg yolk in a bowl then add 2 tablespoons granulated sugar. Whisk until smooth and fluffy.

Pour fresh milk into a pan then bring to boil.

Once it is boiled, pour the hot milk into the egg mixture then whisk slowly until incorporated.

Stir in whipped cream, vanilla extract, and maple syrup. Stir well and strain the mixture.

Pour the mixture into the custard cups with caramel then cover each cup with aluminum foil.

Arrange the cups on the trivet then close the pressure cooker with its lid and seal properly.

Select the menu to high pressure and set time to 6 minutes.

Once it is done, naturally release the pressure cooker then remove the lid.

Take the cups out from the pressure cooker then let them cool.

Chill the cups for at least 4 hours or overnight.

Run a sharp knife around the cups and flip the flan on a serving dish.

Garnish with whipped cream then serve.

Made in the USA
Lexington, KY
26 December 2016